'THE THINKING MAN'S IDIOT'

The Wit and Wisdom
of Boris Johnson

'THE THINKING MAN'S IDIOT'

The Wit and Wisdom
of Boris Johnson

Compiled by
A. Vasudevan

Illustrations by Tom Hughes

First published in 2008 by New Holland Publishers (UK) Ltd
London • Cape Town • Sydney • Auckland

10 9 8 7 6 5 4 3 2 1

www.newhollandpublishers.com
Garfield House, 86–88 Edgware Road, London W2 2EA, UK
80 McKenzie Street, Cape Town 8001, South Africa
Unit 1, 66 Gibbes Street, Chatswood, NSW 2067, Australia
218 Lake Road, Northcote, Auckland, New Zealand

ISBN 978 1 84773 359 7

Publishing Director: Rosemary Wilkinson
Publisher: Aruna Vasudevan
Editor: Kate Parker
Editorial Assistant: Cosima Hibbert
Artworks: Tom Hughes
Design and cover design: Vanessa Green, The Urban Ant Ltd.
Production: Melanie Dowland

Printed and bound by Athenaeum Press Ltd, Gateshead, United Kingdom

Note: The author and publishers have made every effort to contact copyright holders.
They will be happy to add any missing citations in future editions of this book.

CONTENTS

L OVE HIM or hate him, everyone knows Boris.

'King of gaffes', 'master of buffoons', Boris Johnson is more than just a bumbling idiot or an intelligent man masquerading as a fool. Boris is a 21st-century icon – a man whose face and figure have graced many a broadsheet newspaper and magazine cover, whose words and misdemeanours have been quoted and reported by commentators around the world.

This collection features many of the best and most well-known 'Borisms'. The title, 'The Thinking Man's Idiot', is not a personal indictment of Boris but is borrowed from the words of the brilliant radio host and jazz great Humphrey Lyttelton (1921–2008) and is just one of many fine quotes in this collection, both by Boris himself on many different subjects, and also about Boris – the man, his views and his appearance – by a wide range of people.

I would like to thank several people: the team at New Holland, particularly Julia Shone, Cosima Hibbert, Kate Parker and Melanie Dowland; also Tom Hughes for his brilliant illustrations; Richard for always believing that anything is possible and inspiring others to believe the same, and last, but certainly not least, Boris Johnson himself, whose humour, wit and social and political commentary have made this book possible.

– A. Vasudevan

BORIS ON
BORIS

'[I am] A wise guy playing
the fool to win.'

–From *The Sunday Times*, 16 July 2000

'Hello, I'm your MP. Actually no, I'm your candidate. Gosh.'

—While canvassing in Henley in 2005

'He may seem like a lovable buffoon but you know he wouldn't hesitate to line you all up against a wall and have you shot.'

–Jeremy Hardy on Radio 4

_____

'It is better to have a serious man being a buffoon than a buffoon pretending to be a serious man.'

–Andrew Gilligan, *Evening Standard*

Conservative Central Office fights hard to
keep willful, excitable blond on a tight leash

'I think if I made a huge effort always to have a snappy, inspiring soundbite on my lips, I think the sheer mental strain of that would be such that I would explode.'

–Quoted in 'Boris leads the Conservative charge',
BBC Newsbeat, 6 May 2008

*'He's the sort of person who
200 years ago would have died
aged 30 leading a cavalry
charge into a volcano.'*

–Comedian Frankie Boyle on BBC2's satirical show,
Mock the Week

'There may be a reason I can't think of but
the problem with that reason is that
I can't think of it now.'

–From the BBC show *Have I Got News For You*

'...people always ask me the same question, they say, "Is Boris a very, very clever man pretending to be an idiot?" And I always say, "No."'

–Political commentator Ian Hislop on the television chat show *Parkinson*, first broadcast on 19 November 2006

Ardal Conyngham, Belfast:

'How can somebody as fat as you get so many good looking women to find you attractive?'

Boris Johnson:

'This strikes me as a trick question.'

—From 'Boris Johnson: you ask the questions', the *Independent*, 1 January 2007

After being called a 'chinless tosser' by an irate passerby, Boris
replied that he didn't mind being called a tosser but 'chinless'
wasn't fair as he had a fine selection of chins

'I could not fail to disagree with you less.'

—Have I Got News For You, 12 December 2003;
also the winner of the Plain English Campaign's
'Foot in Mouth' Award, 2004

'Boris Johnson [is] known as the thinking man's idiot.'

–Commentator and jazz aficionado Humphrey Lyttelton
on the BBC Radio 4 show *I'm Sorry I Haven't a Clue*

'I can hardly condemn UKIP as a bunch
of boss-eyed, foam-flecked euro hysterics,
when I have been sometimes not far short
of boss-eyed, foam-flecked hysteria myself.'

–From 2004, quoted in 'Did I say that?',
the *Observer*, 13 April 2008

'All he's got going for him is fun straw hair and toffish insouciance.'

–Writer Blake Morrison, the *Guardian*, 1 May 2008

*'Boris was told to engage his brain
before speaking in future.'*

–A Conservative Party official, quoted in 'Black Dog',
Mail on Sunday, 12 September 2004

'My hair has yet to induce epilepsy
and cost considerably less than
£400,000 to design.'

—Commenting after his hair was compared
to the new London 2012 Olympic logo, 9 June 2007

'Everyone keeps telling me the whole bumbling idiot routine is just that, a routine that's brilliantly thought through. I'm not so sure. I think that Boris could be a bit of a Chancy Gardener (the simpleton played by Peter Sellers in Being There*).*

Nobody can be that moronic, surely?'

—Cooper Brown, *Belfast Telegraph*, 13 September 2007

'My ambition silicon chip has been
programmed to try to scramble up this ladder,
so I do feel a kind of sense that I have got to.'

–To Sue Lawley on BBC Radio 4's *Desert Island Discs* in 2005

'*Boris Johnson is the person to lead this country back into the 17th century.*'

–Comedian Paul Merton on the BBC television show
Have I Got News For You, quoted in the *Independent*,
9 September 2006

'I've always known my life
would be turned into a
farce, I'm just glad it's
been entrusted to two
such distinguished
men of letters.'

–Boris Johnson in a letter to Toby Young, co-author
(with Lloyd Evans) of 'Who's Your Daddy?',
a play based on Boris's life

*'The priapic Bozza
is pure party Viagra.'*

–Society magazine *Tatler*'s comment on why Boris
topped its annual list of the 100 most invited guests.
Reported in the *Daily Mail*, 5 July 2008

An excited Boris hears a remake of *The Stud* is on the cards

BORIS ON
HIS CAREER

'Will I throw my hat into the ring?
It depends on what kind of ring it is
and what kind of hat I have in my hand.'

—On being asked by the *Oxford Mail* if he would stand
for leader of the Conservative Party

'Try as I might, I could not look at an overhead projection of a growth profit matrix, and stay conscious.'

–Commenting on his first job at a management consultancy,
Herald (Glasgow), 13 November 2004

'Boris Johnson in the role of mayor would feel like being trapped on the set of The Wizard of Oz minus the soundtrack and the Technicolor.'

–Bonnie Greer, writer, the *Guardian*, 1 May 2008

'I will go on hunger strike and throw myself in front of the next horse at Ascot ... Failing that I was going to say I'll sleep with him, but he'd probably say yes.'

–Arabella Weir, actor and writer, on what she would do if Boris were elected Mayor of London, the *Guardian*, 1 May 2008

'Dark Forces dragged me away
from the keyboard, swirling forces of
irresistible intensity and power.'

—Explaining why his work at the *Daily Telegraph* was usually late,
The Sunday Times, 16 July 2000

'I think the possibility is so remote,
it's more likely that I would be blinded
by a champagne cork, decapitated by a
Frisbee or locked in a disused fridge.'

–To Lynn Barbour, the *Observer*, 5 October 2003,
on being asked if he was going to be the next
editor of the *Daily Telegraph*

'They wanted me to get up at the absolute crack of dawn to go milking. In retrospect I probably should have done it. I do know which end of a cow to pull, roughly speaking – if you see what I mean.'

–On standing as candidate for Clwyd South West, 1997. Quoted in 'Did I say that?', the *Observer*, 13 April 2008

'The other day I was giving a
pretty feeble speech when it went off the
cliff and became truly abysmal ...
I began some guff-filled sentence with the
words, "I am sure we all agree..."
It seemed to go well, so I did it again ...
at which point a man down the table shot
to his feet and shouted "Well, I don't!
I don't agree with what you are saying
at all. It seems to me to be quite wrong for
you to claim that we all agree when I don't
agree." And blow me down, he appeared
to be wearing long purple vestments ...
I realised I was being heckled by a
blooming bishop, and from that moment
on my speech was irretrievable.'

– *The Spectator*, 27 January 2007

'*I'd sooner vote for a dog
than Boris Johnson.
Cartoon characters should
only run cartoon cities.*'

–Writer Charlie Brooker commenting on whether Boris should run
for Mayor of London, the *Guardian*, 1 May 2008

'Tremendous, little short of superb.
On cracking form.'

—On being asked how he felt after being sacked
by leader of the Conservative Party, Michael Howard,
The Times, 15 December 2004

'I'm making absolutely no comment ...
and no, I did not.'

—In 2004, on being asked if he intentionally misled
Michael Howard, leader of the Conservative Party

A contemplative Boris compared being fired to finding himself 'ker-plonked' on the ground with his propeller buried in tarmac

'I have successfully ridden two horses for quite a long time. But I have to admit there have been moments when the distance between the two horses has grown terrifyingly wide, and I did momentarily come off.'

−Commenting on his public downfall
from political office in 2004 to Sue Lawley on BBC Radio 4's
Desert Island Discs in 2005; also quoted in the *Observer*, 30 October 2005

'All politicians in the end are like crazed wasps
in a jam jar, each individually convinced
that they are going to make it.'

–To Sue Lawley on BBC Radio 4's
Desert Island Discs in 2005

'My chances of being PM are about
as good as the chances of finding
Elvis on Mars, or my being
reincarnated as an olive.'

—On being asked 'Admit it: you want to become
prime minister, don't you?' by Amanda Findlay of Bolton;
from 'Boris Johnson: you ask the questions',
the *Independent*, 17 June 2004

'I have as much chance
of becoming Prime Minister
as being decapitated
by a Frisbee or of finding Elvis.'

–Boris's response to school children after being asked
whether he wanted to become PM. Also voted the funniest
political quote in the last 50 years in a poll held by
UKTV History to celebrate the launch of Andrew Marr's
A History of Modern Britain (2008)

'I'm backing David Cameron's campaign out of pure, cynical self-interest.'

–'Conference Diary', the *Independent*, 5 October 2005

'If Johnson were elected? I'd feel that he had neither the acumen nor the gravitas to resist becoming the teddy bear of the 4x4-driving, Laura Ashley headscarf-wearing, inherently inegalitarian and snobbish denizens of Chelsea. I'd feel that we had a buffoon as mayor instead of a reptile, and whatever my disagreements with Livingstone – and they are legion – at least he understands what a swamp this city is.'

–Writer Will Self commenting on Boris standing as Mayor of London, the *Guardian*, 1 May 2008

'If there are any dogs in the manger,
then I will have those dogs
humanely euthanased [*sic*].'

–From his first mayoral speech, commenting on
his staff's loyalty, reported in *The Times*, 5 May 2008

'Ach. That floppy hair, and that sodding bicycle. Has any man ever before managed to persuade such a huge number of people that he was a decent chap on two such flimsy, trivial, irrelevant, modish pieces of ephemera?'

–Writer Zoe Williams on the possibility that Boris might be Mayor of London; from 'Be Very Afraid', the *Guardian*, 1 May 2008

'Boris as mayor?
Lovely to see other comedians
getting work, but four years is
a bit long for a comedy routine.'

–Comedian David Mitchell commenting on whether Boris should be
Mayor of London, the *Guardian*, 1 May 2008

'I would like to thank first the vast multitudes who voted against me – and I have met quite a few in the last nine months, not all of them entirely polite ... And as for those who voted for me ... I will work flat out to repay and to justify your confidence ... Where there have been mistakes we will rectify them. Where there are achievements we will build on them. Where there are neglected opportunities we will seize on them ...

Let's get cracking tomorrow and let's have a drink tonight.'

–From his acceptance speech on being elected Mayor of London, 3 May 2008

'Every day I wake up with a sense of wonderment that I'm Mayor of London.

Obviously I realise that other people may also feel a little wonderment.'

–Mayor Boris, or BoJo as he is popularly known, August 2008

'Just three more doors to go!' thinks Boris

BORIS ON
MODERN LIFE

'We can be as nice as pie, we can take our ties off and breakdance down the esplanade and all wear earrings and all the rest of it. It won't make any difference to the electorate if they don't think we're going to offer a new and improved, basically Conservative approach to government'.

—At the Conservative conference, 2005

'This year's going to be even bigger, better
and generally more funkapolitan.'

–Mayor Boris in July 2008, commenting on the 44th
Notting Hill Carnival

'A set of cornrows would sort that flyaway barnet out.'
Boris receives some hairstyling tips

'I'm kicking off my diet with a cheeseburger – whatever Jamie Oliver says, McDonald's are incredibly nutritious and, as far as I can tell, crammed full of vital nutrients and rigid with goodness.'

–While campaigning at McDonald's
in Botley, Oxford, England, May 2005

'What's my view on drugs?
I've forgotten my view on drugs.'

–During the 2005 general election campaign trail

'I think I was once given cocaine but I
sneezed and so it did not go up my nose.
In fact, I may have been doing icing sugar.'

–Response to being asked about drugs in 2005 on the BBC show
Have I Got News For You; quoted on the BBC website in
'The Boris Johnson Story', 4 May 2008

'I'm very attracted to it.
I may be diverting from Tory Party
policy here, but I don't care.'

—On 24-hour drinking legislation, Andrew Pierce,
The Times, 30 April 2005

'I didn't see it, but it sounds barbaric.
It's become like cock-fighting; poor dumb
brutes being set upon each other by
conniving television producers.'

–On *Big Brother*, the *Observer*, 20 June 2004

Boris's campaign for the youth vote gets off to a flying start

'I think what we had there was the kind of exuberant, Celtic-style wake for the passing – the long overdue passing – of a custom.'

–Commenting on the protests by drunken revellers against the imminent ban on drinking on London public transport, June 2008

'Here we are, in one of the most
depressed towns in Southern England,
a place that is arguably too full of drugs,
obesity, underachievement and
Labour MPs.'

–Boris commenting on Portsmouth in 2007

'It's an attested fact that under Conservative governments the quality of living of the British people has immeasurably improved, leading to better denticians, higher calcium consumption ... leading inexorably to superior mammary glands.'

—In 2005; quoted in 'Did I say that?', the *Observer*, 13 April 2008

'Voting Tory will cause your wife to have bigger breasts and increase your chances of owning a BMW M3.'

—During the 2005 election campaign; quoted in 'Boris Johnson ... in his own words', the *Guardian*, 16 July 2007

BORIS ON
SPORT

'What I would advise
fans is to expect little and
possibly they'll receive even less.'

–On England vs Germany:
the Legends match, 3 May 2006

'I'm a rugby player, really, and I knew
I was going to get to him, and when
he was about two yards away I just
put my head down. There was no malice.
I was going for the ball with my head,
which I understand is a legitimate
move in soccer.'

–On headbutting German midfielder Maurizio Gaudino
in the groin during the England vs Germany: the Legends
football match, 3 May 2006

'I love tennis with a passion.
I challenged Boris Becker to a
match once and he said he was
up for it but he never called back.
I bet I could make him run around.'

−*Express*, 21 March 2005

'Ok, I said to myself as I sighted
the bird down the end of
the gun. This time,
my fine feathered friend,
there is no escape.'

–From *Friends, Voters, Countrymen*

'I'm like a greased panther, a coiled spring, all that suppressed kinetic energy.'

—On England vs Germany:
the Legends match, 3 May 2006

BORIS ON THE WORLD

'It is often immigrants who like
waving flags and receiving CBEs,
and they certainly seem
to be good at cricket.'

–On the pros and cons of immigration,
The Sunday Times, 29 January 2006

'We were led to believe that Granny Butter had immensely distinguished French or Alsation antecedents. When I say Alsation, I mean from Alsace, not that they were dogs.'

—Commenting on his family history on the BBC1 programme *Who Do You Think You Are?*, first broadcast 20 August 2008

'I think the trouble is it makes us look very, very pathetic and poodle-like. Here you've got Blair going up to Bush, being summoned by Bush and asking whether he can go to the Middle East, volunteering to go as Bush's emissary to the Middle East and being rejected. And Bush says, "Well Condi's going, don't you worry." And then Blair says again, "Why don't I go, Condi needs a result, I can just talk." And again, he gets turned down. That gives us a rather unfortunate picture of a subservient relationship between us and the United States. There's no question about it.'

—From a transcipt of an interview with the Australian Broadcast Corporation, 24 July 2006

'We in the Tory Party have become used to Papua New Guinea-style orgies of cannibalism and chief-killing, and so it is with happy amazement that we watch as the madness engulfs the Labour Party.'

After a public outcry, Boris said:

'I meant no insult to the people of Papua New Guinea, who I'm sure lead lives of blameless, bourgeois domesticity in common with the rest of us. My remarks were inspired by a Time Life book I have which ... show[s] relatively recent photos of Papua New Guinean tribes engaged in warfare, and I'm fairly certain that cannibalism was involved.'

–Both from 'Johnson sparks diplomatic row over "cannibalism" jibe', the *Independent*, 9 September 2006

BORIS ON TRANSPORT

'Pedestrians are having to sprint at 1.2m
per second to get across the road.'

–Commenting on traffic light phasing, first Mayoral question time,
May 2008

'I seemed to be averaging a speed of X and then the M3 opened up before me, a long quiet Bonneville flat stretch, and I am afraid it was as though the whole county of Hampshire was lying back and opening her well-bred legs to be ravished by the Italian stallion.'

–On driving a Ferrari,
Life in the Fast Lane

'She was blonde. She was beautiful.
She was driving some poxy little Citroen
or Peugeot thing ... And she had just
overtaken me ... And let me tell you,
I wasn't having it. Because if there is one
thing calculated to make the testosterone
slosh in your ears like the echoing sea and
the red mist of war descend over your
eyes, it's being treated as though you are
an old woman by a young woman ...
the whole endocrine orchestra said:
"Go. Take." You can't be dissed by
some blonde in a 305.'

–On driving an Alfa Romeo,
Life in the Fast Lane

'Nor do I propose to defend the right to talk on a mobile while driving a car, though I don't believe [that it] is necessarily any more dangerous than the many other risky things that people do with their free hands while driving – nose-picking, reading the paper, studying the A–Z, beating the children, and so on.'

–In 2002, on driving while on a mobile phone; quoted in the *Guardian*, 1 May 2008

'It might not happen every day.
It will happen but I can't promise it will
be all the time.'

–On wearing a cycle helmet, in June 2008

'I am carrying out a timetable of doom.'

—On his bid to phase out London's unpopular
bendy buses, 2008

BORIS ON
OTHER PEOPLE

'I think the reason there is all this beastliness towards Gilligan is because he is not particularly good looking.'

–Following *The Spectator*'s offer of a job to Andrew Gilligan. Reported in the *Guardian*, 11 February 2004

'We are confident in our story and will be fighting this all the way. I am sorry that Alastair Campbell has taken this decision but I can see that he got his tits in the wringer.'

–On Campbell's negative reply to *The Spectator*'s report that the government had influence on the Queen Mother's funeral arrangements, *Herald*, 24 April 2002

Question from Tom Scarsdale by email:

'You confessed to having had a crush on Polly Toynbee. What is it about Polly that seems to drive Tory boys wild?'

Boris Johnson:

'Oh lord. It's just she's so bossy and posh. Is that the right answer?'

—From 'Boris Johnson: you ask the questions', the *Independent*, 1 January 2007

'My psychological inertia is nothing compared to the quivering invertebracy of these Labour plotters.'

–On the plight of Prime Minister Gordon Brown, July 2008

'Gordon Brown has got lots of things going against him. He's a nail-biting, gloomadon-popping, anxious, high-taxing, high-spending, bossying, nannying, interfering kind of Scot and Blair's got much more user appeal to Middle England.'

–From a transcript of an interview with the Australian Broadcasting Corporation, 24 July 2006

'The President is a cross-eyed Texan warmonger, unelected, inarticulate, who epitomises the arrogance of American foreign policy.'

—Unsigned editorial entitled 'Infantile resentment',
The Spectator, 22 November 2003

'I have not had an affair with Petronella.
It is complete balderdash. It is an inverted
pyramid of piffle. It is all completely
untrue and ludicrous conjecture.
I am amazed people can write this drivel.'

–Denying accusations of an affair with Petronella Wyatt in
November 2004

'But here's old Ken – he's been crass, he's been insensitive and thuggish and brutal in his language – but I don't think actually if you read what he said, although it was extraordinary and rude, I don't think he was actually anti-Semitic.'

–*The Times*, 17 February 2005

Weakest Link finalist flummoxed by particularly
tricky question on bendy buses

'Howard is a dynamic performer on
many levels. There you are. He sent me
to Liverpool. Marvellous place.
Howard was the most effective Home
Secretary since Peel. Hang on,
was Peel Home Secretary?'

—*The Times*, 19 April 2005

'The Lib Dems are not just empty. They are a void within a vacuum surrounded by a vast inanition.'

—uncredited

'I'd want to get Blair and really
interrogate the guy. I'd really want
to pin him up against a palm tree
and slap him around and get the
truth out of him about a few things.'

—uncredited

A great fan of Tony Blair, Boris once referred to him as a cross between Harry Houdini and a greased piglet

Boris's life

1964 Born Alexander Boris de Pfeffel Johnson on 19 June in New York.

1969 Moves to England; attends schools in Camden, London, followed by the European School in Brussels, Ashdown House in East Sussex, and finally Eton College.

1983 Studies classics at Balliol College, Oxford.
Becomes President of Oxford Union and member of the infamous Bullingdon Club (along with David Cameron).

1987 Marries Allegra Mostyn-Owen on 5 September; divorced in 1993.

1988 Joins *Daily Telegraph* as leader and features writer.

1989 Becomes the *Daily Telegraph*'s European Community correspondent.

1993 Marries Marina Wheeler, daughter of journalist Charles Wheeler, with whom he has four children: Milo, Theo, Laura and Cassia.

1994 Becomes assistant editor of the *Daily Telegraph*.

1995 Becomes political columnist for *The Spectator*

magazine.

1997 Unsuccessfully contests Clywd South seat for the Conservative Party.

1998 Begins association with BBC news show *Have I Got News for You*. He eventually racks up the most appearances on the show, alongside Ken Livingstone.

1999 Becomes editor of *The Spectator*.

2001 Elected Conservative MP for Henley-on-Thames.

2004 Appointed Conservative Shadow Minister for the Arts. Later dismissed over alleged affair with fellow *Spectator* journalist.

2005 Re-elected as a MP; resigns from *The Spectator*.

2006 Appointed Conservative spokesperson for high education by David Cameron.

2007 Stands as Conservative candidate in Mayor of London race against Ken Livingstone.

2008 Ousts Ken Livingstone from position to become Mayor of London on 2 May.

Books by Boris

Fiction
Seventy-Two Virgins, Harper Perennial, 2004

Collections and nonfiction
Friends, Voters, Countrymen, Harper Perennial, 2001
Lend Me Your Ears, Harper Perennial, 2004
Have I Got Views For You, Harper Perennial, 2006
Life in the Fast Lane, Harper Perennial, 2007
The Dream of Rome, Harper Perennial, 2007

Books about Boris

Andrew Gimson, *Boris: The Rise of Boris Johnson*, Pocket Books, 2006

Web

www.boris-johnson.com (official site)
www.boriswatch.com (Boris Watch)

About the author

A. Vasudevan is a London-based writer and editor.